A Histor[y of]
World Religions

A concise Guide to the History and Beliefs of Religions Throughout Time

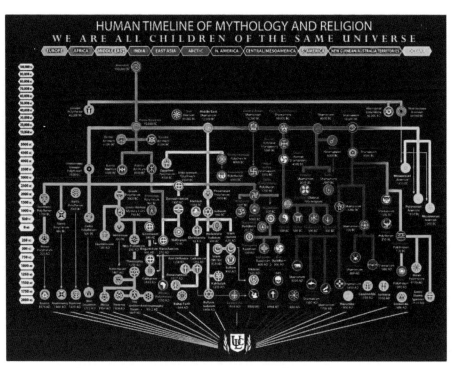

https://www.ulc.org/about/religion-history

Gil Barrett

Table of Contents

Table of Contents

Table of Contents

Table of Contents

What Is Religion?

The answer seems straightforward but can quickly become complex and murky the further down you dig. Some religions follow a classic definition, where they give answers to life's biggest questions, give guidance on how to live a good life, and offer a sense of community through worship.

Other religions resemble philosophy with no places of worship, no priests, and only a vague sense of community that's not fully realized until centuries later when scholars are looking back at them.

Some religious scholars have characterized religion as a belief in spirits or some other form of transcendent life. This idea holds that Animism is the mother of all religions and the chart on the title page is constructed around this idea.

This idea isn't universally accepted. Other scholars hold that religion is about communities and what they value. The beliefs and practices of a religion are just an expression of their values and what they hold sacred or holy.

The religions discussed in this brief history are by no means all of the religions of the world. There are over 4,000 religions that we know of which would make a complete history several thousand pages long.

The religions here are the ones listed in the chart which was provided by the ULC Ministry. Some of the dates in this book will differ from what the chart says because when a religion was founded can often be tricky or controversial. You can find the chart at: https://www.ulc.org/about/religion-history.

Animism

In Animism,
Nature Has Agency

Founded: 100,000 BCE, Global
Area of influence: Global
Holy Books: None
Important Figures: Various
Holidays: Various
Believers: Unknown
Core Beliefs: Animism
Main Practices: Nature Worship

Considered by some to be the foundation of all the religions of the world, Animism is the belief that the natural world is alive and inhabited with spirits.

In this worldview, stones and mountains have personalities, trees and mushrooms have subjective experiences, and animals have a spirit working within them.

The social world which Animist societies inhabit included waterfalls and rivers. People would maintain relationships with the individual persons of the natural world like a tree or flower.

Because Animism is found worldwide, it can be difficult to pinpoint what exactly is common between all Animist beliefs. Modern scholars depict it as the perception of agency in nature.

Polytheism

The Assembly of Gods around Jupiter's Throne
Giulio Romano

Founded: 40,000 BCE, Global
Area of influence: Global
Holy Books: Various
Important Figures: Various
Holidays: Various
Believers: Unknown
Core Beliefs: Multiple Gods
Main Practices: Worship

Polytheism is the general name given to the ancient religions that believed in multiple gods. The Greek Pantheon, the gods and goddesses of ancient Egypt, the religion of the Mayans. In all of them there are multiple deities, though one may be supreme.

The gods and goddesses are generally the divine personification of natural and social forces. The Sky Father, such as Zeus or Tengri, is one. The god of love, war, beauty, storms, and the ocean are other examples.

Oftentimes the gods played a role in the creation of the world and the movement of the seasons and other natural phenomena are attributed to their activities. Worshippers would worship gods to gain favor in whatever realm of life they ruled over.

Shamanism

Founded: ~12,000 BCE, Global
Area of influence: Global
Holy Books: Varied
Important Figures: Varied
Holidays: Varied
Believers: Unknown
Core Beliefs: Animism, Interconnection Of Everything
Main Practices: Spirit Communication, Ancestor Worship, Divination

Mongolian Shaman
Performing a Ritual

The ancient religious art of Shamanism can be found in cultures all around the world, many of which would never have had contact with each other.

The practice revolves around the central figure of the shaman. Shamans were often selected at a young age to undergo rigorous training and education before they became shamans officially.

Shamans were very important figures in their societies. They helped cure the sick, brought abundance of crops or game, escorted souls through death, and travelled to the spirit world to bring back prophecies and other forms of divination.

Shamanism as a modern phenomenon is closely associated with the neo-pagan movement and has only minor similarities.

Atenism

Founded: ~1,348 BCE, Egypt
Area of influence: Egypt
Holy Books: The Great Hymn To The Aten
Important Figures: Akhenaten
Holidays: Unknown
Believers: Unknown
Core Beliefs: Monotheism
Main Practices: None

Akhenaten Giving Offerings
to Aten With His Family

Competing with Zoroastrianism for the title of the world's first monotheistic religion, Atenism was a short-lived experiment of the Egyptian pharaoh Akhenaten.

The trouble in describing Atenism is that, despite being so ancient, it was virtually unknown until the 19th century. This was because later Egyptians viewed Atenism as something heretical and removed all mentions of its existence.

What made Atenism such a revolution from its precursor Egyptian Polytheism was that Aten, the solar aspect of Ra, became the source of all other gods and thus the only god. Aten was also too distant to contact, making prayer and priests irrelevant except Akhenaten who saw himself as Aten's son.

Hinduism

The OM Symbol

Founded: ~1,500 BCE, India
Area of influence: South Asia
Holy Books: The Vedas, The Smritis
Important Figures: Swami Vivekananda, Mahatma Gandhi
Holidays: Diwali, Holi, Vaisakhi
Believers: 15 Million
Core Beliefs: Karma, Brahman, Atman
Main Practices: Artha, Kama, Moksha, Darshana, Meditation

Known as the Sanatana Dharma, or Eternal Faith, Hinduism is less of a religion and more of a way of life. It describes many different cultures in South Asia with no universal dogma or religious leader.

That isn't to say that Hinduism is just Indian or Nepali culture. Hindus believe that the entire universe is one immanent but transcendent Supreme Being named Brahman. Everything that exists is Brahman. Individuals have souls that are called Atman, but they are of the same essence as Brahman.

Atman are immortal and live in the material world of suffering known as Samsara. Karma is the law of cause and effect and it keeps our Atman separate from Brahman until we achieve Moksha, where our karmic debts are paid and we reunite with Brahman.

In the material world, there are three manifestations of Brahman, known as the Trimurti. Brahma is the creator of the universe, Vishnu is the preserver, and Shiva is the destroyer. The lifespan of the universe is separated into four Yugas, wherein the Trimurti create, preserve, and eventually destroy the universe.

The four primary denominations of Hinduism are Saivism, Shaktism, Vaishnavism, and Smartism.

Statue of Shiva

5 Zoroastrianism

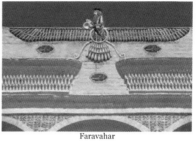

Faravahar
Symbol of Zoroastrianism

Founded: ~1100 BCE, Persia
Area of influence: Global
Holy Books: The Avesta
Important Figures: Zarathushtra
Holidays: Naw-Ruz, Yalda
Believers: ~150,000
Core Beliefs: Monotheism, Dualism
Main Practices: Ritual, Magic, Astrology

Sometimes called the world's first monotheistic religion, Zoroastrianism emerged from Persian polytheism.

Zoroastrians believe that Ahura Mazda is the one true god. In Persian polytheism, Ahura Mazda was at the top of a pantheon of gods.

In Zoroastrianism, Ahura Mazda (The Lord of Wisdom) and his enemy Ahriman are pitted in a cosmic battle of good and evil. The good is destined to win and the world will return to a perfect state of being on the day of judgment, when evil is no more.

These ideas have influenced countless religions that followed it. Zoroaster is also considered the father of astrology and magic. It is the world's oldest living religion.

Jainism

The Logo of Jainism

Founded: ~1,000 BCE, India
Area of influence: India
Holy Books: The Agams, The Purvas
Important Figures: Mahavira
Holidays: Paryushana, Diwali
Believers: 4 Million
Core Beliefs: Nontheism, Reincarnation, Karma
Main Practices: The Five Vows

One of the major Indian Vedic religions, Jainism came into being around the same time as Buddhism as part of a larger trend away from Hinduism.

Jains practice the Five Vows in the pursuit of attaining Enlightenment and liberation from Samsara. The Five Vows include nonviolence, chastity, honesty, not stealing, and non-attachment. Nonviolence is particularly important to Jains.

There are two sects of Jainism, the Digambara and the Svetambara. The Digambara are the more orthodox of the two. They are called sky-clad because their monks reject materiality to the point of going naked. The Svetambara are white-clad, so called for their white robes. One difference is that Svetambara believe women are capable of achieving Enlightenment.

Judaism

Founded: 950 BCE, Jerusalem
Area of influence: Global
Holy Books: The Tanakh, The Talmud
Important Figures: Abraham, Moses, Judah
Holidays: Passover, Yom Kippur, Hanukkah, Sabbath
Believers: 15 Million
Core Beliefs: Monotheism, Messianism
Main Practices: The 613 Mitzvahs, Halakhah

Young Man Wearing a Kippah
and Reading the Torah

Judaism is the first of the Abrahamic religions to form and thus one of the oldest living religions. It is a monotheistic religion, one of the first in existence.

The core of Judaism revolves around the Covenant that God made with Abraham. In this covenant, God promises Abraham a land of their own, the Promised Land. His children will be prosperous and God will do great works through them.

In return, they must follow the law written down in the Torah. In one sense, Judaism is the religion of Abraham's descendants adhering to Jewish Law in keeping with this promise.

Judaism is a messianic religion, believing that one day a Jew will become the savior of humanity. This is in fact how Christianity was born, as Jesus Christ is claimed to be this messiah. Judaism preaches that when the messiah comes, the world will know no death or suffering. Because there is suffering, Christ is not seen as the messiah.

The Tenakh is the Hebrew Bible, containing the Torah, the Neviim, and the Ketuvim. The Talmud, sometimes called the Oral Torah, is a compilation of rabbinical discourses.

Synagogue in Sofia, Bulgaria

⁷ Greco-Roman Mystery Cults

Founded: ~750 BCE, Greece and Rome
Area of influence: Greece and Rome
Holy Books: None
Important Figures: Plato
Holidays: None
Believers: Unknown
Core Beliefs: Polytheist
Main Practices: Initiation, Psychedelics

Fresco in Pompeii Depicting
the Mystery Cult of Dionysus.

As one might expect of a mystery cult, the Greco-Roman Mysteries are shrouded in well, mystery.

Generally speaking, the various mystery cults were semi secret initiatory societies that focused on a single deity in the Greek or Roman pantheon.

The most famous of these is the Eleusinian mysteries, which worshiped Demeter. Through ritual use of psychedelics, they worshipped the reaping and sowing of grain. Revealing the secrets of the mystery was punishable by death.

Other major mystery cults included the Dionysian and Orphic mysteries. The mysteries had an important role to play in the religious evolution of the area and influence religions even today.

Taoism

Taoism Yin Yang Icon

Founded: ~500 BCE, China
Area of influence: East Asia
Holy Books: Tao te Ching, The Daozang
Important Figures: Lao-tzu, Chuang-tzu
Holidays: The Lantern Festival, Tomb Sweeping Day
Believers: 9 Million
Core Beliefs: The Tao
Main Practices: Wu-Wei, Meditation, Alchemy, Yangsheng

Taoism refers to a wide range of Chinese beliefs that don't fit neatly into a single description. The Tao is often translated as the Way or Path. Taoism is a practical, concrete set of instructions on how to align oneself with the Tao.

The Tao can be described as the source of all creation and also the natural course along which the universe moves. Through self-cultivation, Taoists strive to live more spontaneously and with less resistance to the world. This is called Wu-Wei or nonaction.

The Taoist sages are perfected beings with access to the creative energy of the very universe. In so doing, they become fearless, vital, and wise.

Buddhism

Buddhist Monks

Founded: 5th c. BCE, India
Area of influence: Global
Holy Books: Pali Canon (Tripitaka)
Important Figures: Siddhartha Gautama
Holidays: Vesak, Māgha Pūjā, Parinirvana Day
Believers: 500 Million
Core Beliefs: Four Noble Truths, Karma, Nontheism, The Middle Way
Main Practices: Meditation, Mindfulness, Individual Study

Although there are many Buddhas, Buddhism was founded by the Buddha Siddhartha Gautama. Buddha is a title that means The Awakened One, referring to Siddhartha's state of Enlightenment.

The Buddha's teachings center around the Four Noble Truths, which concern the nature of suffering and the path one must travel to be free from suffering.

The worldview of Buddhism is highly complex but put simply, they believe that we live in Samsara, a cyclic existence of suffering. The Buddha's teachings aim to help people reach Nirvana, a state of non-suffering characterized by egolessness.

Buddhism is as much a spiritual practice as it is a religion proper, and one of the Buddha's major contributions was the Middle Way. Having been raised as a prince before living life as an ascetic, he came to the conclusion that the path to Enlightenment is a balance between ascetic self-denial and hedonic self-indulgence.

Although most of the world's Buddhists live in Asia, the late 20th century saw a significant increase in interest in the West. Western Buddhism currently has more in common with Mahayana Buddhism but will undoubtedly evolve into something unique as it matures.

Painting of Buddha at Wat Preah Prom Rath
Siem Reap, Cambodia

Shinto

Founded: ~500 BCE, Japan
Area of influence: Japan
Holy Books: None
Important Figures: Izanagi, Izanami
Holidays: Seijin Shiki, Rissun, Shichigosan
Believers: 100 Million
Core Beliefs: Kami
Main Practices: Kami Veneration, Purification

Shinto Shrine in Hokkaido

Shinto is the Japenese ritualistic worship of Kami, or spirits. Shin means gods or spirits and To is the same Way as the Tao in Taoism.

Shinto is more of a practice than a religious set of beliefs. There are no holy books or set of beliefs to follow. Instead there are shrines which the vast majority of Japanese people visit regularly for ritual purification and veneration of the Kami.

Shinto priests are in charge of keeping the shrines clean and for performing rituals at the shrine. Anyone can become a priest if they choose.

Shinto coexists with Buddhism in Japan. Shinto is the source of daily ritual and practice while Buddhism gives insight into death and the afterlife.

Confucianism

Founded: ~500 BCE, China
Area of influence: China
Holy Books: The Five Classics
Important Figures: Confucius
Holidays: Confucius' Birthday, Chinese New Year
Believers: 6 Million
Core Beliefs: Education, Family, Ritual
Main Practices: Moral Self-Cultivation, Ancestor Worship

Statue of Confucius

Developed during the Warring States Period in China, Confucianism is primarily a doctrine of good social norms and structures.

Confucianism does reference theology at times which makes it a religious philosophy but there is an ongoing debate over whether Confucianism is a philosophy of life or a religion proper.

Education is a primary focus of Confucianism as Confucians believe that teaching young children good morals and ethics will lead to a healthier and more prosperous society.

The family is also important, with the government being structured in a similar way as the family structure. Confucians also practice ancestor worship.

Hellenistic Judaism

Founded: ~300 BCE, Greece
Area of influence: Middle East
Holy Books: The Tanakh
Important Figures: Philo
Holidays: Traditional Jewish Holidays, Naw Ruz
Believers: Unknown
Core Beliefs: Monotheism, Syncretism
Main Practices: Contemplation, Prayer

Philo As Imagined by Andre Thevet

Hellenistic Judaism is the title given to the ideas of Jews living in the Greek empire, particularly in Alexandria, Egypt and Antioch, Syria. The title is not universally accepted but is useful for giving a name to a very influential period of religious thought.

In short, Hellenistic Judaism was the child of Judaism and Greek philosophy, in particular the ideas of Plato, Pythagoras, and the Stoics.

One notable theologian from this period was Philo of Alexandria, whose attempt to reconcile Jewish thought with the Greek philosophers is indicative of the group.

His concept of God as a transcendent but imminent being that does not resemble humans was picked up by the Gnostics and the Neoplatonists. Their level of influence on later religious thought is impressive for the length of time they existed.

Hellenism

Founded: ~300 BCE, Egypt
Area of influence: Middle East
Holy Books: Unknown
Important Figures: Unknown
Holidays: Easter,
Believers: Unknown
Core Beliefs: Monotheism, Hellenist Philosophy
Main Practices: Contemplation, Prayer

Alexander the Great

Just as Greek polytheism and philosophy had an impact on Judaism in the Greek empire of Alexander the Great, after Alexander's Greek religion became influenced by the melting pot of religions that the region had created.

Hellenism as it is referred to here is not the same as Greek Polytheism nor is it the neopagan religion by the same name. Hellenism here refers to the particularly multicultural blend of religious thought in the late Greek empire.

Hellenism had a major impact on the religion of the Roman empire, which would come to replace it.

Tengrism

Founded: ~300 BCE, Mongolia
Area of influence: Central Asia
Holy Books: None
Important Figures: Tengri
Holidays: Nardugan, Nowruz
Believers: ~300,000
Core Beliefs: Animism, Shamanism, Totemism, Monotheism
Main Practices: Ancestor Worship

Tengrist Symbol

Tengrism is the Central Asian religion that developed out of shamanism and is centralized in Mongolia and Turkey. Tengri is the supreme God, making Tengrism a monotheistic religion, but there are many demigods and spirits that exist as well.

In Tengrism, practitioners aim to live in harmony with nature. By living in harmony with nature and being a morally upright person, you perfect your Wind Horse or soul.

Tengri is a Sky-Father deity and the monotheistic aspect of his worship did not occur until later in the history of Tengrism. Eje is Mother Earth and serves alongside Tengri.

Through animal sacrifice and other forms of worship, Tengrist shamans act on behalf of the people to have Tengri grant them favors and cure them of illnesses.

Theravada Buddhism

Theravada Monk

Founded: ~250 BCE, India
Area of influence: Southeast Asia
Holy Books: Pali Canon
Important Figures: Buddhagosa
Holidays: Traditional Buddhist Holidays
Believers: 125 Million

Theravada is more ascetic than Mahayana. Renouncing civilian life and becoming a monk or nun is characteristic of the practice, with notable demarcation between practitioners and laypeople.

There moral life of the practitioner is emphasized, although study and practice are still of primary importance. The goal is to become an Arhat (akin to a saint-scholar), not to become a Buddha yourself.

Due to its monastic practices and adherence to the Pali Canon, Theravada is the more orthodox school. Its teachings are simple and focus on individual liberation from suffering.

Theravada is alternatively referred to as Hinayana, or Lesser Vehicle. The title is sometimes considered pejorative, though not always or even usually. Theravada is the only school of Hinayana which has survived.

Mithraism

Founded: 70 BCE, Rome
Area of influence: Mediterranean
Holy Books: The Book Of The Two Principles
Important Figures: Mithras
Holidays: Unknown
Believers: Unknown
Core Beliefs: Unknown
Main Practices: Initiation

Stele of the Tauroctony,
Mithras Sacrificing a Bull.

Mithraism is one of the Roman mystery cults. It was popular in the first century CE, which made it a competitor to Christianity.

Although Mithraism as a social gathering was not secretive, no Mithraic literature has survived to the present day. This makes it difficult to tell what these people believed and did.

Mithraism was likely a voluntary social gathering, not unlike the Freemasons today. Members came together in decorated caves called Mithraeum to explore the mysteries of 'the descent of souls and their exit back out again.'

Mithras, not to be confused with the Persian god Mithra, was a sun god. The Mysteries of Mithras centered around astrological signs and their initiates had a patron planet depending on which of the seven tiers of hierarchy they were on.

Mahayana Buddhism

Founded: 1st c. CE, India
Area of influence: Global
Holy Books: Pali Canon
Important Figures: Nagarjuna, Asanga
Holidays: Traditional Buddhist Holidays
Believers: 350 Million

Golden Temple Kushalnagar
Karnataka, India

Translated as the Greater Vehicle, Mahayana encompasses many schools of Buddhism including Zen and Pure Land. In Mahayana, the goal is to become a bodhisattva, one who works to awaken all living beings not just themselves.

There is an emphasis on the development of prajna (wisdom), which leads the practitioner to realize shunyata (emptiness). This realization gives insight into egolessness which is used to foster compassion toward all living beings, the mark of a bodhisattva.

The Madhyamaka school, founded by Nagarjuna, is centrally focused on the study of his teachings on emptiness and the Middle Way. Asanga's Yogachara school is the second major Mahayana school. It teaches that consciousness alone exists.

Christianity

Jesus Christ

Founded: 33 CE, Jerusalem
Area of influence: Global
Holy Books: The Bible
Important Figures: Jesus Christ
Holidays: Christmas, Easter, Lent, All Saint's Day, Advent
Believers: 2.2 Billion
Core Beliefs: Monotheism, The Trinity, Salvation
Main Practices: Eucharist, Prayer, Baptism

Christianity is the second of the Abrahamic religions and revolves around the figure of Jesus Christ. Christ is actually a title, not a name, and designates Jesus as the Messiah.

Christians believe that we once lived in the Garden of Eden, where we walked with God. But then we sinned and were kicked out of God's presence. This Original Sin is the reason humanity suffers.

The purpose of life for the Christians is to devote themselves to prayer and repentance, relying on Jesus to absolve them of their wrongdoings so they will be accepted back into Heaven after they die.

Before Jesus was killed by crucifixion, he taught his twelve disciples how to live a life closer to God. The Golden Rule, which underlies Christian ethics, says to treat others the way you want to be treated.

Today, Christianity is the most popular religion in the world with almost a third of the global population identifying as Christian.

Empty tomb of Jesus at sunrise with crosses

Hermeticism

Hermes Trismegistus

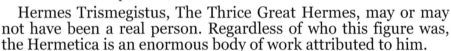

Founded: ~100 CE, Egypt
Area of influence: Global
Holy Books: The Hermetica
Important Figures: Hermes Trismegistus
Holidays: None
Believers: Unknown
Core Beliefs: Monism, Sympatheia, Human Divinity
Main Practices: Episteme, Gnosis

Hermes Trismegistus, The Thrice Great Hermes, may or may not have been a real person. Regardless of who this figure was, the Hermetica is an enormous body of work attributed to him.

The ideas expressed in the Hermetica have had an immense influence on religious thought. It is often associated with Occultism, for example the Hermetic Order of the Golden Dawn, but has had an impact on almost all religious thought.

In essence, Hermes taught that the world is one and that the one is God. The human being is a microcosm of the divine world and as such has the capacity to interact with God and to come to know God's mind, or Nous.

Gnosticism

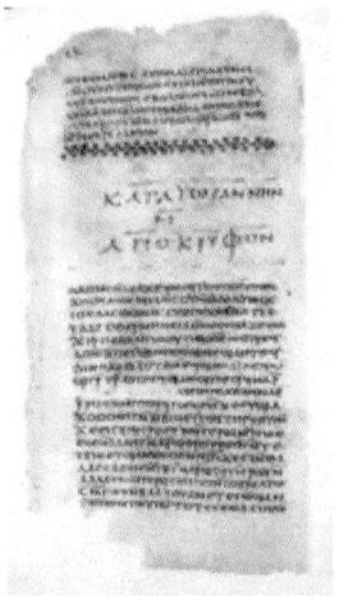
Nag Hammadi Codex 2

Founded: 2nd c. CE, Middle East
Area of influence: Middle East, Europe
Holy Books: Nag Hammadi Library
Important Figures: Jesus Christ
Holidays: Unknown
Believers: Unknown
Core Beliefs: Duality, Salvation Through Christ
Main Practices: Asceticism, Contemplation, Baptism

Gnosticism is a term that was later used to describe a variety of religious schools of thought which thrived in the 2nd and 3rd centuries CE.

The primary group of Gnostics were the Sethians which gave rise later to the Valentinians. Gnosis is personal acquaintance with God, and that is the highest calling of the Gnostic.

The Gnostic cosmology is highly complex. Ultimately, there is a divine world outside of time called the Pleroma. The material world we live in is the creation of Yaldabaoth, the Demiurge, the ignorant and often cruel god of the Old Testament.

The Gnostics believe that Jesus is the messiah sent from the One, or the God beyond Being. Through Christ's teachings, we can realize the divine within us and revolt against Yaldabaoth. It is similar to Christian orthodoxy but also quite different.

Neoplatonism

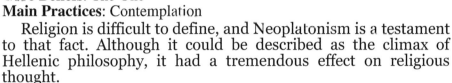

Plotinus

Founded: ~245 CE, Rome
Area of influence: Global
Holy Books: None
Important Figures: Plotinus, Plato
Holidays: None
Believers: Unknown
Core Beliefs: The One
Main Practices: Contemplation

Religion is difficult to define, and Neoplatonism is a testament to that fact. Although it could be described as the climax of Hellenic philosophy, it had a tremendous effect on religious thought.

It owes its outsized influence to its core belief in the One. The One is a belief in the absolute unity of the universe, whose source is absolute Consciousness (Meister Eckhart would later term this the Godhead).

This profound theory's influence cannot be overstated and, although Neoplatonism is a modern term, its course through history would take a much larger text than this.

Manichaeism

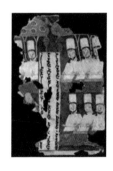

The Elect

Founded: 3rd c. CE, Persia
Area of influence: Europe, Middle East, Asia
Holy Books: The Manichaean Heptateuch
Important Figures: Mani
Holidays: Bema Festival, Yimki
Believers: Unknown
Core Beliefs: Duality, Syncretism
Main Practices: Asceticism, Prayer

Founded by Mani in a religious melting-pot dominated by Zoroastrianism, Manichaeism is sometimes called the first world religion because it reached from Spain to China.

Mani considered himself a follower of all the religious leaders, but first and foremost of Jesus Christ. As such, Manichaeans considered themselves Christians, despite Christian persecution.

Manichaeism is associated with extreme duality. Light is good and darkness is evil. The world is the product of darkness attacking the light. Humans are beings of light trapped in a universe of darkness.

Through strict asceticism and fasting, the Elect (the clergy) purge themselves of darkness with the help of the Hearers (laypeople).

Islam

Muhammad's Name

Founded: 610 CE, Saudi Arabia
Area of influence: Global
Holy Books: Quran
Important Figures: The Prophet Muhammad
Holidays: Ramadan, Eid, Hajj
Believers: 1.8 Billion
Core Beliefs: Monotheism
Main Practices: Prayer, Fasting, Pilgrimage To Mecca, Sharia

The second largest religion in the world, and the fastest growing religion in the world, Islam is centralized around two beliefs: Belief that Allah is the one and only God and that the prophet Muhammad was his messenger.

There are many different sects of Islam but the two major ones are Sunni and Shia. The divide started after Muhammad died in 632 CE and had to do with Muhammad's successor, the first Caliph or leader of Islam.

Sharia, which means 'path to water', is the name for Islamic law but more generally refers to the basic guidelines of how to be a good Muslim. Sharia is not set in stone and there are many interpretations of what it includes.

Generally speaking, there are five pillars of being a good Muslim, although different sects disagree on the number. These include a statement of faith, prayer, fasting, charity, and a pilgrimage to Mecca known as Hajj.

The Kaaba in Mecca, Saudi Arabia

Shi'ite

Imam Mosque
Isfahan, Iran

Founded: 632 CE, Middle East
Area of influence: Iran, Pakistan, India, Iraq
Holy Books: Quran
Important Figures: Muhammad, Ali, Husayn
Holidays: Ramadan, Eid, Hajj
Believers: 150 Million
Core Beliefs: Monotheism
Main Practices: Prayer, Fasting, Pilgrimage To Mecca, Sharia

Making up about 15% of all Muslims, the Shia are so called because they were supporters of Muhammad's cousin and son-in-law Ali.

At the time of Muhammad's death, the Shiat Ali (Party of Ali) believed that Muhammad had declared Ali to be his successor. The controversy surrounding this dispute and other claims to power led to the Ridda (apostasy) wars.

There are many similarities between the different sects of Islam but Shia Muslims are known for the succession of religious scholars called the Twelve Imams.

Iran is the most prominent Shia nation but Shia Muslims also hold dominance in several South Asian countries.

Sunni

Prophet's Mosque
Medina, Saudi Arabia

Founded: 632 CE, Middle East
Area of influence: Global
Holy Books: Quran, Sunnah, Hadith
Important Figures: Muhammad, Abu Bakr
Holidays: Ramadan, Eid, Hajj
Believers: 1.7 Billion
Core Beliefs: Monotheism
Main Practices: Prayer, Fasting, Pilgrimage To Mecca, Sharia

Sunni Islam is the most popular form of Islam, with nearly 80% of the Muslim world being Sunni. Sunna is often translated as the way or the trodden path and refers to the teachings and practices of Muhammad and his contemporary followers.

After Muhammad died in 632 CE, the group that became the Sunni believed that the next leader of Islam was to be decided democratically and that Abu Bakr, Muhammad's close friend, won that election.

One distinguishing feature of the Sunnis is their use of Hadith. Hadith are sayings of Muhammad as told by people around Muhammad. These sayings are considered strong or weak depending on their isnad, or chain of transmission. The closer the chain to Muhammad, the more trustworthy the saying.

Vajrayana Buddhism

Founded: ~600 CE, India
Area of influence: Tibet
Holy Books: Tantras
Important Figures: Padmasambhava, Kukai
Holidays: Traditional Buddhist Holidays
Believers: ~20 Million

Hevajra Mandala

Also known as the Diamond Vehicle, Vajrayana is the highest form of Buddhist practice. It is traditionally accepted that mastery of both the Hinayana and Mahayana is required before attempting Vajrayana practice.

It is known as the Diamond Vehicle because it focuses on that which is indestructible in you, namely your buddha nature. Through the tantric practices of meditation, yidams, and mantras, the student of Vajrayana aims to achieve enlightenment within a single lifetime.

Vajrayana is more esoteric than the Hinayana or Mahayana and its teachings are notoriously difficult to understand, which is why a guru is essential for its practice. Vajrayana is practiced primarily by the four schools of Tibetan Buddhism and the Japanese Shingon school.

Sufism

Founded: 7th c. CE, Arabia
Area of influence: Africa, South Asia
Holy Books: Quran
Important Figures: Junayd al-Baghdadi, Rumi
Holidays: Ramadan, Eid, Hajj
Believers: 9 Million
Core Beliefs: Monotheism, Mysticism
Main Practices: Prayer, Fasting, Asceticism

Whirling Dervish Show
Konya, Turkey

The founding of Sufism is a matter of historical dispute but is most commonly associated with Islamic mysticism. Through an ascetic rejection of the mundane, physical world, Sufis seek to reunite with God or at least to grow near to God.

As an example, one prominent Sufi named Al-Hallaj experienced a spiritual reverie in which he proclaimed "I am the Truth" which in Arabic is the same as saying "I am God." He was executed for this heresy, but his martyrdom in the name of spiritual unity with God, or Allah, is indicative of the group.

The popular Sufi poet Rumi and his followers started the Mevlevi Order, famous for the Whirling Dervishes. Dervishes are ascetic Muslims who engage in ecstatic rituals such as dance.

Tibetan Buddhism

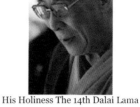

His Holiness The 14th Dalai Lama

Founded: 7th c. CE, Tibet
Area of influence: Himalaya Region
Holy Books: Pali Canon
Important Figures: Songtsen Gampo, Atisha
Holidays: Traditional Buddhist Holidays
Believers: ~15 Million

Tibetan Buddhism is made up of four schools: Nyingma, Kagyu, Gelug, and Sakya. The current Dalai Lama, the spiritual leader of Tibet, comes from the Gelug school.

It is generally understood by Buddhists that Buddhism cannot be separated from the culture it is in. Tibetan Buddhism is no different, and influences from the pre-Buddhist Tibetan religion Bon are evident.

The Tibetans take the monastic lifestyle of Theravada, mix it with the intellectual power of the Mahayana, and hold the tantric practices of Vajrayana as the highest form of practice.

After the Dalai Lama was exiled in 1959 by the Chinese Communist Party, many Tibetan Buddhists fled the country and began teaching around the world.

Bogomilism

The Bogomil Symbol KOLOVRT
On a Tombstone in East Serbia.

Founded: 940 CE, Bulgaria
Area of influence: The Balkans
Holy Books: The Secret Supper, Visions Of Isaiah
Important Figures: Bogomil, Basil The Physician
Holidays: None
Believers: Unknown
Core Beliefs: Dualism
Main Practices: Asceticism, Vegetarianism, Celibacy

The Gnostic spiritual offspring of Manichaeism and Paulicianism, Bogomilism is a dualistic Christian heresy.

Bogomils believed that the world was created by Mammon, the devil. Because the material world is a thing of evil, the way to god is world-renunciation.

Bogomilism was very popular with poor Balkans, as its leaders were strongly anti-institutional. Bogomili lived ascetically, rejecting anything that tied them to the physical world including alcohol, meat, and sex.

Bogomilism was heavily condemned by the Catholic church. Hungary invaded Bosnia, where Bogomilism was the state religion, twice because of the Catholic crusade.

Catholicism

The Vatican

Founded: July 16, 1054, Jerusalem
Area of influence: Global
Holy Books: The Bible
Important Figures: The Pope
Holidays: Traditional Christian Holidays
Believers: 1.3 Billion
Main Practices: Liturgy, Confession

Catholicism traces its history back to when Jesus was alive but became the church it is today in The Great Schism when it officially broke from the Eastern Orthodox church.

Many people know Catholicism through the Pope. The Pope is the bishop of Rome and is considered the spiritual successor to the Apostle Paul through apostolic succession.

The Vatican is the center of Catholicism. It is a city-state in Rome, ruled by the Pope. The Vatican is home to the Sistine Chapel and centuries' worth of treasures and artifacts.

Catholics make up roughly half of all Christians worldwide.

Eastern Orthodox

St. Alexander Nevsky Cathedral

Founded: July 16, 1054, Jerusalem
Area of influence: Eastern Europe
Holy Books: The Bible
Important Figures: Michael Cerularius
Holidays: Traditional Christian Holidays
Believers: 200 Million
Main Practices: Worship, The Sacred Mysteries

The Great Schism, which divided Catholicism from Eastern Orthodox, is why we have Christian denominations today. Orthodox translates to 'right belief' which is emblematic of the theological differences which led to the division.

Although Eastern Orthodox Christians still believe in Jesus Christ, they are distinct from the other main denominations in that they are considerably more mystical in their approach.

Unlike the Western denominations, the Eastern Orthodox Church uses the Septuagint. The Septuagint is an early Greek translation of the Bible but notably includes the Apocrypha.

Catharism

Founded: 1143 CE, Germany
Area of influence: Western Europe
Holy Books: The Book Of The Two Principles
Important Figures: Jesus Christ
Holidays: Unknown
Believers: Unknown
Core Beliefs: Duality, Reincarnation
Main Practices: Asceticism, Veganism, Celibacy

Cathars Cross in France

Because of its doctrinal similarities, Catharism is speculated to be a descendant of the Manichaeans and Gnostics. It has many similarities with Bogomilism, whose priests endorsed Catharism publicly in its early years.

Catharism is a dualistic religion, believing that there are two principles of divinity instead of the orthodox Holy Trinity of Catholicism. The good half of the divine is God, the creator of the spiritual realm. The devil is the creator of the physical world.

There were two levels for most Cathars, the perfect and the believers. Through a ritual known as the consolamentum, believers were initiated into the group of the perfect.

The perfect followed strict rules of asceticism, veganism, and celibacy. The believers were held to a lighter standard.

Kabbalah

Founded: ~1270 CE, Spain
Area of influence: Global
Holy Books: The Zohar a.k.a. The Book Of Radiance
Important Figures: Moses de Leon, Moses Cordovero
Holidays: None
Believers: Unknown
Core Beliefs: Ten Sefirot, Feminine Divine Power
Main Practices: Prayer,

The Ten Sefirot In the Allegory of the Tree

Kabbalah is less a religious subsection of Judaism, such as Reform Judaism, than it is a grouping of influential ideas within Jewish Mysticism.

Generally speaking, Kabbalah is about Ein Sof or God as Infinity. The uncreated being without end which we all exist within. The world was created by a contraction within Ein Sof.

The material world is connected to Ein Sof through the ten Sefirot, or manifestations of God. The Sefirot are often expressed in an allegory of a tree.

The ideas of Kabbalah have had an immense influence on religious thought since their creation, not the least of which being Western spiritual organizations such as the Golden Dawn.

Sikhism

Founded: ~1500 CE, Punjab
Area of influence: Global
Holy Books: Guru Granth Sahib
Important Figures: Guru Nanak
Holidays: Vaisaki, First Parkash, Hola Mohalla
Believers: 25 Million
Core Beliefs: Monotheism
Main Practices: Initiation, The 5 K's, Naam Japna, Langar

Sikh Temple Sri Harmandir Sahib
Punjab, India

Also known as Sikhi, Sikhism is one of the fastest growing religions in the world. Sikhs place a strong emphasis on their Gurus, with Guru Granth Sahib being the founder of the religion.

Sikh places of worship are called Gurdwara, which means Gateway to the Guru, and their holy scripture is called Guru Granth Sahib which is treated as a living Guru. All Gurdwara contain a copy of the Guru Granth Sahib.

There is a strong emphasis on community. Langar is the practice of feeding the community, regardless of religious affiliation or caste.

Sikhs believe in a God that is all things, we are all a part of this One and our individual egos are an obstacle to realizing this.

Protestantism

Founded: October 31, 1517, Wittenberg, Germany
Area of influence: Global
Holy Books: The Bible
Important Figures: Martin Luther, John Calvin
Holidays: Traditional Christian Holidays
Believers: 800 Million to 1 Billion
Main Practices: Baptism, Communion

Martin Luther

The Protestant Reformation began when Martin Luther, a German monk, nailed his 95 Theses to the door of All Saint's Church in Wittenburg, Germany.

At its core, the Reformation was a response to the increasingly political and secular Catholic church. Luther was excommunicated shortly after, in 1521.

Such diverse denominations as Evangelicalism and Calvinism are called Protestant because they were founded during this period of protest.

The defining features are the beliefs that we are saved through faith and not deeds and that each Christian has direct access to God.

Macumba

Founded: 1550 CE, Brazil
Area of influence: South America
Holy Books: None
Important Figures: Unknown
Holidays: Lady of Aparecida Day
Believers: Unknown
Core Beliefs: Monotheism, Orishas
Main Practices: Ritual, Prayers, Offerings, Magic

An Offering to Orishas

Macumba is the name given to the Afro-Brazilian religions which were created when Africans were brought to the region. In some respects, it is the Brazilian equivalent of Voodoo.

Within Macumba there are three different sects: Umbanda, Candomblé, and Quimbanda. Umbanda and Candomblé have their own sections in this book. Quimbanda is considered the black magic sect because it deals with evil (or careless) spirits.

Practitioners of Macumba are monotheistic because they believe that Olodumare is the supreme deity but Olodumare is distant and doesn't interact with our world.

Orishas are lesser gods and spirits and practitioners of Macumba give offerings to them in order to gain some favor or benefit or to curse someone else.

Candomblé

Founded: 1550 CE, Brazil
Area of influence: Brazil
Holy Books: None
Important Figures: Olodumare
Holidays: Lady of Aparecida Day
Believers: Unknown
Core Beliefs: Monotheism, Orishas
Main Practices: Ritual, Prayers, Offerings, Dance

Candomblé Group
Salvador, Bahia, Brazil

Popular in the Brazilian state of Bahia, Candomblé is the closest to the African Yoruba traditions of the Macumba sects. Through music and dance, members enter into trance-like states where they can interact with the orishas.

Members of Candomblé also give offerings to the orishas such as plants or animals. By giving offerings, they can ask for advice or favors.

A primary concern in Candomblé is healing. The spirit can become unwell and members heal their spirit by getting in contact with their orisha.

Candomblé is a closed tradition and much of their teachings are transferred orally.

Santeria

Santeria Practitioner
Old Havana, Cuba

Founded: ~1550 CE, Cuba
Area of influence: Cuba, Mexico, The U.S.
Holy Books: None
Important Figures: Olodumare
Holidays: Feast of Obatala, Babalú-Ayé's Birthday
Believers: 75 Million
Core Beliefs: Monotheism, Orishas, Syncretism
Main Practices: Ritual, Prayers, Divination, Initiation

The Afro-Cuban religion of Santeria draws from the Yoruba traditions of West Africa and the Catholicism of the Europeans in Cuba. Santeria is sometimes called La Regla Lucumi.

Olodumare is the Creator god who manifests as three divinities. One of these deities, Olofi, is tasked with teaching humanity how to live good and moral lives. The Orishas, spirits or saints, are Olofi's messengers and act as intermediaries.

A trained priest, called a babalawo, initiates members in a ritual called Ifa. Through this ritual, members discover which Orisha is in charge of them. Through worship and devotion, members gain insight from their Orisha who protects them, guides them, and gives them assistance.

Haitian Voodoo

Woman In Trance
Gonaives, Haiti

Founded: 17th c., Haiti
Area of influence: South and North America
Holy Books: None
Important Figures: Dutty Boukman, Marie Laveau
Holidays: Feast of Ogou St. Jacques, All Saint's Day
Believers: 60 Million
Core Beliefs: Monotheism, Lwa (Spirits)
Main Practices: Sevis Lwa (Service To The Spirits)

Voodoo is the popularized term for Voudon or Vodou. Practitioners of Voodoo are called Voduisants.

Bondye is the creator God in Voodoo. Bondye is unavailable to humans, but lwa are spirits who act as his intermediaries. The practice of Voodoo centers around sevis lwa, or service to the spirits including ancestor worship.

Sevis lwa involves animal sacrifice and other offerings to the spirit for protection or some other benefit. With the help of an oungan (male priest) or manbo (female priest), voduisants will enter a trance and become possessed by an lwa. The beneficial rite of passage allows the lwa to give advice to other voduisants.

25 Neo Druidism

Awen

Founded: 1780s, England
Area of influence: Europe, North America
Holy Books: None
Important Figures: Ross Nichols, Isaac Bonewits
Holidays: The Eight Sabbats (Wheel Of The Year)
Believers: ~40,000
Core Beliefs: Pantheism
Main Practices: Nature Worship

Another faction of the neo-pagan movement, Neo Druidism is a return to pre-Christian Celtic traditions. It began in the late 18th century when Iolo Morganwg, a Welsh poet, forged historical texts regarding Welsh history.

Although not historically accurate, he began a process through which Neo Druidism came to exist today. There are many different modern Druid societies, including Ár nDraíocht Féin and the Order of Bards, Ovates and Druids.

Neo Druids emphasize getting in touch with nature and worship according to the seasons. They practice rituals to bring themselves closer to nature, including Gorsedd which are large open gatherings with bards and spirits.

Hoodoo

High John the Conqueror
Hoodoo Saint

Founded: ~1800 CE, The United States
Area of influence: The United States
Holy Books: The Bible, Pow-Wows
Important Figures: Black Hawk, John the Conqueror
Holidays: Lady of Aparecida Day
Believers: Unknown
Core Beliefs: Magic, Spirits,
Main Practices: Ancestor Worship, Rituals, Healing

Hoodoo, also called Conjure or Rootwork, was born out of the fragmented spiritual traditions of the American South. It is considered a closed practice which belongs to the lineage of African Americans.

Practitioners, often called root doctors, hoodoo doctors, and conjure men or women, act as community healers and spiritual teachers.

Although the terms are not easily distinguished, generally speaking conjure refers to working with angels, saints, or the spirits of the dead. Rootwork is associated with healing through herbalism and alchemy.

Hoodoo is largely an oral tradition and as such, its teachings are difficult to come across if you are not in the tradition.

Reform Judaism

Founded: July 17, 1810, Germany
Area of influence: Global
Holy Books: The Tanakh, The Talmud
Important Figures: Rabbi Abraham Geiger
Holidays: Traditional Jewish Holidays
Believers: ~1.8 Million
Core Beliefs: Monotheism, Messianism
Main Practices: Prayer, Halakhah

Hebrew Star of David

In the early 19th century, as the ghettos Jews lived in were being closed down and they were allowed to enter into Christian society, many of them felt the need to modernize their faith in order to gain acceptance and retain congregants.

Over the past 200 years of its existence, Reform Judaism has undergone a number of changes. Today, in what is called Modern Reform Judaism, one can describe the movement as the progressive wing of Judaism.

Popular especially in the United States, Reform Judaism teaches acceptance of all people regardless of race, gender, or sexuality.

In contrast to Orthodox Jews, who see Jewish Law as binding, Reform Jews see it as subject to ethical considerations.

Mormonism

Founded: April 6, 1830, New York
Area of influence: Global
Holy Books: The Bible, The Book of Mormon
Important Figures: Joseph Smith, Brigham Young
Holidays: Christmas, Easter, Pioneer Day
Believers: 16.8 Million
Core Beliefs: Monotheism, The Trinity, Salvation
Main Practices: Word Of Wisdom, Missionary Work

The Salt Lake Temple

The Church of Jesus Christ of Latter Day Saints is its formal name, but many people refer to this religion as Mormonism.

Mormonism emerged from the Protestant ferment known as the Second Great Awakening. Its unique flavor of Christianity stems from its having four books of scripture, instead of just one.

The Book of Mormon tells the purported history of the Native Americans, including a visit from Jesus Christ after his death in Jerusalem but before his Ascension.

The leader of Mormonism is called the Prophet and is believed to have a direct connection with God.

Ayyavazhi

The Symbol of Ayyavazhi

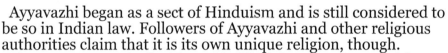

Founded: 1840 CE, India
Area of influence: India
Holy Books: Akilattirattu Ammanai, Arul Nool
Important Figures: Ayya Vaikundar
Holidays: Kodiyettru Thirunal, Thiru Eadu Vasippu
Believers: Unknown
Core Beliefs: Monism, Dharma
Main Practices: Neetham, Vinchai, Charity

Ayyavazhi began as a sect of Hinduism and is still considered to be so in Indian law. Followers of Ayyavazhi and other religious authorities claim that it is its own unique religion, though.

There are many similarities with Hinduism, but Ayyavazhi believes that Kali has adulterated the Vedas and that they are not as trustworthy as Hindus believe.

Ayyavahi was founded by Ayya Vaikundar and his writings are considered scripture above the Vedas, although the Vedas are still sometimes used.

In Ayyavazhi, we are all a part of Ayya or the one Supreme Being. Kali is an evil force who has separated us from unity and the pursuit in Ayyavazhi is unification with Ayya once more.

Bahá'í Faith

Bahai Lotus Temple New Delhi, India

Founded: 1844 CE, Persia
Area of influence: Global
Holy Books: The Writings Of Baha'u'llah
Important Figures: Baha'u'llah, The Bab
Holidays: Naw Rúz, First Day of Ridván
Believers: 6 Million
Core Beliefs: Monotheism, World Unity
Main Practices: Prayer, Contemplation, Spiritual Development

The Bahai Faith was founded by Baha'u'llah (Glory of God) who was a Babi, or follower of the Bab (The Gate), whose message was that a new manifestation of God was coming.

Baha'u'llah declared himself to be that messenger. The core belief of the Bahai is the unity of the world. Humans are one people and all of the religions of the world are like chapters in a lesson-book which God is giving to us.

This means that the Buddha, Muhammad, Abraham, Jesus Christ, Zoroaster, and Baha'u'llah are all manifestations of one God.

Bahais are pacifists and preach tolerance and the elimination of prejudice. They pray daily, meditate, and practice spiritual development through contemplation and moral righteousness.

Rosicrucianism

Founded: 1865 CE, Germany
Area of influence: The West
Holy Books: None
Important Figures: Christian Rosenkreuz
Holidays: None
Believers: ~200,000
Core Beliefs: Unknown
Main Practices: Pursuit Of Perfection

Rose Cross

Claiming to be descendants of the ancient Mysteries traditions, the history of the Rosicrucians is difficult to pin down.

Although contemporary incarnations began in the early 1900s, the books which describe its founding were published in the 1600s, and the alleged founding took place in the early 1400s.

Influenced by the Kabbalists, the Christian Gnostics, and the Mystery Traditions, the Rosicrucians have largely kept their beliefs secret.

What we do know is that Rosicrucianism is a mystical tradition that claims access to secret, esoteric knowledge about the laws of the universe. They believe in the personal pursuit of perfection by unifying the spiritual and physical realms.

Theosophy

Founded: 1875 CE, New York City
Area of influence: North America and Europe
Holy Books: None
Important Figures: Helena Blavatsky
Holidays: None
Believers: 50,000 - 100,000
Core Beliefs: The One
Main Practices: Mediumship, Divination, Magic

Helena Blavatsky

Credited with bringing Eastern religious thought to the West, Theosophy is an amalgam of Truth-seekers who embrace comparative religion as a path toward that Truth.

The name Theosophy is roughly translated from Greek as Divine Wisdom. Its practitioners are heavily influenced by the Neoplatonic idea of the One but incorporate Eastern ideas of Enlightenment with Occult practices in their pursuit of Truth.

Its call for common humanity mixed with esoteric thought influenced many later groups, including the New Age movement.

The Golden Dawn

Founded: October, 1887, England
Area of influence: North America, Europe
Holy Books: The Cipher Manuscripts
Important Figures: William Wynn Westcott
Holidays: None
Believers: 100
Core Beliefs: Occult Science
Main Practices: Magic

The Hermetic Order Of
The Golden Dawn

Arguably the greatest occult society of the last two centuries, the Golden Dawn was born out of the Rosicrucian and Theosophical societies.

Three members of the Rosicrucian Society discovered the Cipher Manuscripts and decoded them. What they discovered became the foundation for an esoteric initiatory society that laid the foundation for modern Western Hermeticism.

Through successive stages of training, neophytes would gain the mental strength and occult knowledge necessary to become their highest spiritual selves and enact the universal will through magic.

Umbanda

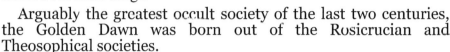

Founded: ~1900 CE, Brazil
Area of influence: South America
Holy Books: None
Important Figures: Zélio Fernandino de Moraes
Holidays: Lady of Aparecida Day
Believers: ~400,000
Core Beliefs: Reincarnation,
Main Practices: Ritual, Prayers, Offerings, Magic

Umbanda Session, The Gira

Zélio Fernandino de Moraes is sometimes credited as the founder of Umbanda, although it's not universally accepted. Regardless, it is a Brazilian syncretic religion which combines Buddhism, Catholicism, Spiritualism, and Candomblé together.

Umbanda is often considered the white magic strand of Macumba whereas Quimbanda is the black magic strand. Since there is no dogma or hierarchy, Umbanda can take many forms.

Umbanda is considered to be a wholly Brazilian religion and has a nationalist flavor. It appeals to the middle class and tends to evolve alongside any religion it comes in contact with.

The Catholic saints and the Yoruba orishas are often seen to be the same entities just with different names. Members with access to the world of the orishas act as intermediaries for laypeople.

Thelema

Founded: 1904, England
Area of influence: North America and Europe
Holy Books: The Book Of The Law
Important Figures: Aleister Crowley
Holidays: Equinox Of The Gods, Thelemic New Year
Believers: Unknown
Core Beliefs: Do What Thou Wilt Shall Be The Whole Of The Law
Main Practices: Magick

Unicursal Hexagram Symbol

A former neophyte in the Golden Dawn, Aleister Crowley founded Thelema when he wrote the Book of the Law. It was written in three days at the dictation of Aiwass, a spirit that visited Crowley through his wife Rose while they were in Egypt.

Crowley is easily one of the most famous occultists of the 20th century. Although Thelema draws from a wider range of occult sciences including the Qabalah and yoga, Crowley's writings are the primary source of knowledge for Thelemites.

The Ordo Templi Orientis (O.T.O.) and the Argenteum Astrum (A.A.) are the largest Thelemite associations. They function as initiatory schools and are still active today.

The Great Work of the Thelemite is to become more in tune with their True Will, akin to discovering your higher purpose.

Anthroposophy

Founded: December 28, 1912, Germany
Area of influence: Global
Holy Books: The Works Of Rudolf Steiner
Important Figures: Rudolf Steiner
Holidays: None
Believers: ~40,000
Core Beliefs: Spiritual Realism, Ethical Individualism
Main Practices: Spiritual Science

Goetheanum in Dornach
Home of the Anthroposophical Society

The first Secretary General of the German Section of the Theosophical Society, Rudolf Steiner, broke away in 1912 to form the Anthroposophical Society.

Anthroposophy is founded around the idea of spiritual development, particularly in childhood. This may be why the Waldorf Schools are so popular, as they are an education system modeled on Steiner's ideas.

In essence, Anthroposophy is the pursuit of developing our body, mind, and spirit. This is done through scientific research in enhanced consciousness and an adherence to self-determination.

³¹ Rodnovery

Kolovrat - Symbol of the Sun

Founded: Early 20th c., Europe
Area of influence: Eastern Europe, Russia
Holy Books: None
Important Figures: Zorian Dołęga-Chodakowski
Holidays: Kupala Night, Koliada
Believers: ~40,000
Core Beliefs: Monism
Main Practices: Ancestor Worship

Otherwise known as the Slavic Native Faith, Rodnovery is another neo-pagan movement based on the pre-Christian Slavic traditions.

Rod is the name for the supreme deity, the creator of the universe. By creator, it is meant that Rod is the source from which all things come, including the lesser gods. This makes Rodnovery a monistic faith.

The Slavic Native Faith is difficult to define socially because many groups exist across many countries, with no central authority figure apart from local priests.

Generally speaking, the worship of ancestors and embracing one's community in nature are the main practices of Rodnovers.

Santo Daime

Mestre Irineu
Santo Daime Founder

Founded: ~1930 CE, Brazil
Area of influence: Global
Holy Books: None
Important Figures: Raimundo Irineu Serra
Holidays: Christmas, Irineu's Birthday
Believers: Unknown
Core Beliefs: Syncretism
Main Practices: Ayahuasca Rituals, Meditation, Dance

Founded by Raimundo Irineu Serra ("Mestre Irineu") in the 1930's, Santo Daime centralizes around the sacrament of Daime which is also known as Ayahuasca.

Daimistas, practitioners, get together for Trabalhos, translated as works. In the Trabalho, Daime is ingested and Daimistas will meditate, engage in ritualized dance, or syng hymns depending on the occasion.

Much of the beliefs of Santo Daime are intended to be experiential, meaning that they are communicated through the experience of taking Daime.

Its message draws from Christianity, New Age spiritualism, South American Shamanism, and African Animism. In general, their message is harmony, love, truth, and justice.

Scientology

Church of Scientology Sign
San Francisco, California

Founded: February, 1954, Los Angeles
Area of influence: United States of America
Holy Books: Dianetics
Important Figures: L. Ron Hubbard
Holidays: Hubbard's Birthday, Auditor's Day
Believers: ~20,000 (Officially: 10 Million)
Core Beliefs: Thetans, Reactive Mind, Reincarnation
Main Practices: Auditing

The Church of Scientology is based off of the writings of former science fiction writer L. Ron Hubbard. His book Dianetics, released in 1950, provides the foundation for Scientology.

Understanding Scientology is difficult due to their secrecy, but the fundamentals are that we are immortal beings called Thetans who are clouded over by the physical world.

Practicing Scientology involves paying thousands of dollars to be audited in the pursuit of Going Clear. Eventually, the practitioner becomes so in tune with their true self that they gain supernatural powers over the physical world.

Wicca

Wiccan Altar

Founded: 1954 CE, England
Area of influence: The West
Holy Books: Book of Shadows
Important Figures: Gerald Gardner
Holidays: The Eight Sabbats
Believers: ~300,000
Core Beliefs: Nature Is Divine, Divinity Is Female And Male
Main Practices: Witchcraft, Rituals, Individual Study

Influenced by Aleister Crowley's magick rituals and Margaret Murray's scholarly studies of medieval witchcraft, Wicca is a neopagan religion that combines earth worship with ritual magic.

Wiccans are a diverse group of people with no central figure of authority. While this leads to a diversity of beliefs, they share in common a few core tenets, such as a belief in reincarnation and a polytheistic belief in many gods and goddesses existing in nature.

Wiccans attribute the highest spiritual authority to the Goddess, which has endeared them to many second- and third-wave feminists.

Eckankar

Symbol of Eckankar

Founded: 1965, USA
Area Of Influence: Global
Holy Books: Shariyat-Ki-Sugmad
Important Figures: Paul Twitchell, Harold Klemp
Holidays: Founder's day, Spiritual New Year
Believers: 50,000 estimated
Core Beliefs: Eck is the holy spirit. Soul travel, dream interpretation
Main Practices: Chanting, soul travel, dream interpretation

Eckankar believes in the Sugmad or god, and that we are all spiritual parts of the one or Eck. In Eckankar, one uses chanting of the sacred word OM, HU, or personal spirit chants to help achieve spiritual travel to the 12 planes of consciousness.

Drawing from Eastern religions, Eckankar believes that the soul is separate from the body and can soul travel to experience other planes of existence to help break the wheel of reincarnation.

They believe that many of the past religious masters, such as Jesus, Lao Tse, and Muhammad were messengers with the same goal in a long line of Eck masters spreading wisdom to their believers through time. The ultimate goal is to achieve self-realization, and God-realization within our lifetime.

Romuva

Romuva Flag

Founded: 1967, Lithuania
Area of influence: Lithuania
Holy Books: None
Important Figures: Jonas Trinkunas, Inija Trinkūnienė
Holidays: Kucios, Kaledos, Rasa
Believers: ~10,000
Core Beliefs: Polytheism, Animism
Main Practices: Dainos, Nature Worship

Hailing from Lithuania, Romuva is the neo-pagan movement reviving the old Baltic gods. Interestingly enough, Romuva has many similarities with the Indian Vedic religions, Hinduism in particular.

The Lithuanian poet-philosopher Vydūnas, writing in the early 20th century, was an active proponent of what would become contemporary Romuva. Its formation has been slow and Romuva has yet to be recognized by the Lithuanian government.

In Romuvan mythology, the world was created by the god Dievas. The storm god Perkunas takes a central role in this mythology, similar to Zeus and Thor. Many Romuvan practices center around nature and fire.

Ásatrú

The Valknut - Odin's Knot

Founded: May, 1973, Iceland
Area of influence: Northern Europe and the US
Holy Books: Poetic Edda, Prose Edda
Important Figures: Sveinbjörn Beinteinsson
Holidays: The Four Solstices
Believers: ~40,000
Core Beliefs: Polytheism, Norse Gods, Animism
Main Practices: Blot, Sumble, Runework

Part of the more general movement known as Heathenry, Asatru is the modern revival of the Old Way (Forn Sidr) of Norse paganism. As a neo-pagan religion, Asatru is reconstructed using the anthropological texts available.

Asatru roughly translates to "being true to the Norse gods," the most famous of which are Odin, Thor, Freyja, Frigg, and Loki. Local worship groups called kindreds, led by a priest (godi) or priestess (gydje), gather together outside to praise the gods and ask for blessings.

Although Asatruar believe in an afterlife, they emphasize personal responsibility, loyalty, and honesty in this life.

Works Cited

Universal Life Church Ministries, "Human Timeline of Mythology and Religion." *Universal Life Church* , 16 Jan., 2023, https://www.ulc.org/about/religion-history

Wladyslaw, "Goetheanum, Dornach, Switzerland." *Wikipedia* , 16 Jan. 2023, https://commons.wikimedia.org/w/index.php?curid=3999348

Frater SEM, "Hermetic Order of the Golden Dawn."
Wikimedia Commons , 16 Jan. 2023, https://commons.wikimedia.org/w/index.php?curid=50996861

All other images are public domain.

ISBN: 9798374263374

Printed in Great Britain
by Amazon

44728531R00027